Energy Transition Strategies for Oil and Gas Companies

Table of Contents

Preface

Introduction

Prelude

Chapter 1: The Need for Energy Transition

Chapter 2: Diversification into Renewable Energy

Chapter 3: Decarbonization and Reducing Carbon Footprint

Chapter 4: Hydrogen as a Clean Fuel Source

Chapter 5: Strategic Partnerships and Collaborations

Chapter 6: Sustainable Business Models and Financial Innovation

Chapter 7: Workforce Transition and Reskilling

Conclusion

Glossary

Preface

The oil and gas industry is at a crossroads, facing unprecedented changes driven by the global energy transition. As the world moves toward cleaner, more sustainable energy sources, companies in the sector are under pressure to adapt quickly to new technologies, stricter environmental regulations, and shifting market dynamics. Recognizing the need for practical, accessible, and forward-looking knowledge, the *Gosships Learning Series* was developed to provide industry professionals with the tools they need to thrive in this evolving landscape.

This series is designed to offer foundational to intermediate knowledge with a focus on actionable strategies that can be implemented in real-world operations. Each book in the series is paired with a certification test, ensuring that the knowledge acquired is not only understood but can also be effectively applied to support business goals and contribute to a successful energy transition.

The *Gosships Learning Series* empowers oil and gas industry personnel, from field workers to corporate managers, by equipping them with the skills and insights necessary to navigate the challenges of the energy transition. We hope this series will support your professional development and help unlock new opportunities for growth and leadership in a low-carbon future.

Introduction

Welcome to the *Gosships Learning Series*, designed to help professionals in the oil and gas sector expand their knowledge and enhance their careers in the context of the global energy transition. This book, titled *Energy Transition Strategies for Oil and Gas Companies*, was developed by industry experts and seasoned executives to provide authoritative and up-to-date insights into the strategies and technologies that are driving the transition to a more sustainable energy future. Whether you are new to the topic or looking to deepen your understanding, this resource will equip you with the knowledge you need to lead your company through this transformative period.

In this book, we will explore the following key areas:

- **Decarbonization Pathways**: Learn about the various strategies oil and gas companies can adopt to reduce their carbon footprint, including carbon capture and storage (CCS), fuel switching, and energy efficiency improvements.

- **Renewable Energy Integration**: Understand how oil and gas companies are diversifying their portfolios by investing in renewable energy sources such as wind, solar, and biofuels.

- **Hydrogen as a Transition Fuel**: Discover the growing role of hydrogen as a cleaner energy alternative, with a focus on its production, storage, and potential applications across industries.

- **Regulatory and Policy Drivers**: Explore the evolving regulatory landscape and how government policies are shaping the energy transition for oil and gas companies.

- **Economic and Market Shifts**: Analyze the financial implications of the energy transition, including the rise of carbon pricing, the decline of fossil fuel demand, and the growing investment in green technologies.

After completing this book, you will be prepared to take an assessment designed to test your comprehension of the material. Upon passing the assessment, you will be eligible to receive a Certificate of Achievement, which can be obtained through www.gosships.com. This certificate will validate your expertise in energy transition strategies and demonstrate your readiness to help guide your organization through the challenges and opportunities of the low-carbon future.

Who Is This Book For?

This book is designed for a wide range of professionals in the oil and gas industry, including:

- **Field Operators and Engineers**: Personnel who need to understand the technical implications of new energy transition technologies and strategies.

- **Corporate and Strategic Managers**: Decision-makers responsible for shaping the future direction of their companies in response to market and regulatory shifts.

- **Aspiring Students**: Individuals seeking to enter the energy sector with a solid understanding of the energy transition and its impact on traditional oil and gas operations.

- **Government and Regulatory Officials**: Professionals working to develop or enforce policies that guide the energy transition in the oil and gas sector.

By mastering the concepts in this book, you will be better equipped to lead your company through the complexities of the energy transition, stay compliant with emerging regulations, and contribute to a more sustainable and efficient energy future.

Thank you for choosing the *Gosships Learning Series* as a resource for your continuous learning and professional development in this critical time of change for the oil and gas industry.

Gosships Learning Series 2024/2025

1. Hydrogen: The Fuel of the Future
2. Green Ammonia: The Next Big Thing in Shipping
3. Decarbonizing Shipping: Pathways to Zero Emissions
4. Battery Technology for Industrial Applications
5. Carbon Capture and Storage: Can It Save the Planet?
6. Biofuels 101: Turning Waste into Energy
7. Understanding LNG (Liquefied Natural Gas)
8. Methanol as a Marine Fuel
9. Offshore Wind Energy: The Future of Renewable Power
10. Tidal and Wave Energy: Harnessing the Ocean
11. Electrofuels: The Next Generation of Carbon-Neutral Fuels
12. Energy Storage Systems for Grid Reliability
13. Hydrogen Fuel Cells for Transportation
14. Solar Energy Innovations: Beyond Solar Panels
15. Smart Grids: The Backbone of Future Energy Systems
16. Ammonia-Hydrogen Blends: A Dual Fuel Solution?
17. Nuclear Power: Small Modular Reactors for a Low-Carbon Future
18. Hydropower: The Oldest Renewable Energy Source
19. Decentralized Energy Systems: Microgrids for Resilience
20. Energy Efficiency Technologies for Industry
21. Hydrogen Production from Seawater
22. Fuel Cells for Maritime Applications
23. Geothermal Energy: Unlocking Earth's Heat
24. Future of EV Charging Infrastructure
25. Synthetic Fuels: Bridging the Gap to Decarbonization
26. Cybersecurity for Maritime and Offshore Operations
27. AI and Automation in Shipping and Logistics
28. Digital Twins in Maritime: Revolutionizing Asset Management

29	Risk Management in Offshore and Maritime Operations
30	Compliance with IMO 2020 Regulations
31	Sustainable Ship Design: Reducing Environmental Impact
32	Marine Renewable Energy: Wave, Tidal, and Offshore Wind Integration
33	Ballast Water Management Systems
34	Blockchain Technology in Shipping: Improving Transpc'y & Efficiency
35	Effective Supply Chain Management for Energy Industries
36	Leadership in the Energy Transition
37	Effective Crisis Management in Maritime Operations
38	Shipyard Safety Management Systems
39	Port State Control (PSC) Inspection Readiness
40	Remote Vessel Operations and Autonomous Shipping
41	Optimizing Fleet Performance with Data Analytics
42	Maritime Environmental Regulations: Staying Ahead of Compliance
43	Advanced Maintenance Strategies: Condition Monitoring & Predictive Maintenance
44	Global LNG Market: Trends and Opportunities
45	Incident Investigation in Maritime Operations
46	International Maritime Law: Key Concepts and Applications
47	Emergency Preparedness and Response for Offshore Oil & Gas
48	Energy Transition Strategies for Oil and Gas Companies
49	Maritime Drones: Applications and Safety Considerations
50	Effective Project Management in Offshore Energy Projects

All Rights Reserved Disclaimer

The contents of this book, including but not limited to all text, graphics, images, logos, and designs, are the intellectual property of Gosships LLC and are protected by copyright law. No part of this publication may be reproduced, distributed, transmitted, displayed, or modified in any form or by any means, including photocopying, recording, or other electronic or mechanical methods, without the prior written permission of the publisher, except in the case of brief quotations in critical reviews or articles.

The information contained within this book is for educational purposes only and is provided "as is" without warranty of any kind, either expressed or implied. The authors and publishers disclaim any liability for any direct, indirect, or consequential loss or damage arising from the use of the material in this book.

For permissions or inquiries, please contact: admin@gosships.com

© 2024 Gosships LLC. All rights reserved.

Prelude

The global energy landscape is undergoing a dramatic transformation. For over a century, fossil fuels—particularly oil and gas—have been the backbone of global energy production. However, mounting concerns over climate change, depleting natural resources, and environmental degradation are compelling the world to transition to cleaner, renewable sources of energy. The shift from fossil fuels to renewable energy is what is referred to as the "energy transition."

This transition is not just a buzzword or an ideological stance but a necessary step to achieve the global climate goals set out in initiatives like the **Paris Agreement**. Oil and gas companies are at the epicenter of this transition. While they have long been synonymous with fossil fuels, their technical expertise, financial power, and infrastructure mean they have the opportunity—and responsibility—to be leaders in the journey toward a low-carbon future.

This mini-book explores how oil and gas companies can adapt to this changing energy landscape through strategies such as diversifying into renewable energy, reducing their carbon footprint, investing in clean technologies like hydrogen, and reskilling their workforce. These strategies will ensure that they not only survive but thrive in the decades to come. The path ahead is challenging, but it is full of opportunities for those willing to embrace change.

Chapter 1
The Need for Energy Transition

1.1 Global Climate Commitments

The increasing urgency surrounding climate change is driving global action to reduce greenhouse gas emissions. This is best reflected in international agreements such as the **Paris Agreement**, which was adopted by nearly 200 countries in 2015. The Paris Agreement's central goal is to limit global warming to well below 2 degrees Celsius above pre-industrial levels, with a more ambitious target of limiting the rise to 1.5 degrees Celsius. To meet these targets, carbon dioxide (CO_2) emissions from burning fossil fuels need to be drastically reduced.

For the oil and gas industry, which is responsible for a significant portion of these emissions, this global commitment presents a clear mandate: decarbonize or face regulatory, financial, and reputational risks. Additionally, there is growing pressure from shareholders, investors, and consumers for companies to align with climate goals. Companies failing to do so may find themselves subject to "carbon divestment" campaigns, where investors pull their money from firms deemed too reliant on fossil fuels.

Many governments have already adopted **net-zero emissions** targets, aiming to eliminate or offset all greenhouse gas emissions by a specific date, often 2050. The adoption of these policies signals to the oil and gas industry that its traditional business model must evolve. These commitments are leading to a surge in regulations targeting carbon emissions, with more expected in the coming decades.

1.2 Regulatory Pressures

Regulatory pressures are ramping up as governments respond to climate change by implementing stricter emissions standards, carbon pricing mechanisms, and incentives for renewable energy development. In Europe, the **European Green Deal** sets a path toward climate neutrality by 2050, which includes revising emissions targets, implementing carbon taxes, and supporting low-carbon technologies. The **European Union Emissions Trading System (EU ETS)**, for example, creates a cap-and-trade market where companies must buy allowances for each ton of CO_2 they emit, adding a financial cost to carbon-intensive operations.

In North America, although regulatory approaches vary by region, states like California have implemented ambitious emissions reduction goals. Additionally, Canada has introduced a **federal carbon tax** that increases over time, directly impacting fossil fuel producers.

In countries like China and India, where oil and gas demand continues to rise, there is still a push for cleaner energy. China, the world's largest carbon emitter, has pledged to achieve **carbon neutrality by 2060**, and it is investing heavily in renewable energy technologies, such as wind and solar power, as well as nuclear energy.

As regulatory frameworks tighten, oil and gas companies must proactively adapt by integrating carbon reduction strategies into their business models. Failing to meet these regulations could result in severe financial penalties and loss of market access, not to mention the reputational damage that comes with being viewed as non-compliant or environmentally irresponsible.

1.3 Market Trends and Consumer Demand

Consumer preferences are shifting toward greener, more sustainable products, and this trend is influencing the energy market. Increasingly, consumers are demanding transparency in how products are sourced and produced, including the energy they use. Companies across sectors are adopting **Environmental, Social, and Governance (ESG)** principles, which prioritize sustainability, ethical practices, and long-term environmental stewardship.

Investors are also playing a pivotal role in this shift. Major investment firms, such as **BlackRock**, have made bold statements about the importance of sustainability in their portfolios, urging companies to align with climate goals or risk losing access to capital. This has led to an increase in **sustainable finance** products like green bonds and ESG-linked loans, which reward companies for reducing their environmental impact.

As a result, oil and gas companies are under pressure not only to diversify into renewable energy but also to ensure that their core operations are as environmentally friendly as possible. Public sentiment is moving in favor of companies that are transparent about their sustainability initiatives, and consumers are increasingly willing to pay a premium for greener products and services.

1.4 Risks of Inaction

Failing to act on climate change and the energy transition presents a range of risks for oil and gas companies, including:

- **Financial Risk**: Carbon-intensive projects may become stranded assets—resources that are no longer profitable to extract due to changes in regulations or market conditions. Additionally, companies that do not adapt may see their costs rise due to carbon taxes or the need to purchase emissions permits.

- **Reputational Risk**: Public perception is increasingly influenced by a company's commitment to sustainability. Companies that lag behind in their transition strategies may face backlash from environmental groups, consumers, and investors.

- **Operational Risk**: As the global energy system shifts away from fossil fuels, oil and gas companies may find it harder to secure contracts, particularly as governments and corporations favor low-carbon energy solutions.

Chapter 2
Diversification into Renewable Energy

2.1 Investing in Renewable Energy

The most obvious strategy for oil and gas companies to participate in the energy transition is to diversify into renewable energy. While fossil fuels will remain part of the global energy mix for some time, there is growing demand for cleaner energy sources, such as solar, wind, and geothermal power. By investing in these technologies, oil and gas companies can reduce their reliance on fossil fuels and tap into rapidly expanding markets.

Companies such as **BP**, **TotalEnergies**, and **Shell** have already begun significant investments in renewable energy projects. BP has announced its aim to reduce its oil and gas output by 40% by 2030 while increasing its renewable energy capacity by 10 times. Shell, similarly, is transitioning toward becoming a major electricity provider, with a focus on solar and wind energy projects, as well as electric vehicle charging infrastructure.

The transition to renewables also aligns with the growing demand for **energy as a service** models, where energy companies sell not just electricity or fuel but solutions that include energy management, storage, and grid integration.

2.2 Building Renewable Infrastructure

Oil and gas companies have the financial strength, technical expertise, and global infrastructure needed to develop large-scale renewable energy projects. For example, many oil and gas companies are uniquely positioned to build and operate offshore wind farms, thanks to their experience with offshore oil platforms and subsea engineering.

The **North Sea** has seen significant development in offshore wind energy, where former oil companies are leading the charge. Offshore wind power is becoming increasingly cost-competitive and is expected to play a major role in the global energy mix. Additionally, offshore wind farms have the advantage of being located in areas with strong, consistent winds, making them highly productive.

Oil and gas companies can also invest in **solar energy** by leveraging their vast land holdings, many of which are located in areas with high solar potential. Additionally, they can incorporate **energy storage solutions**, such as batteries, to help balance supply and demand in renewable energy systems.

2.3 Case Studies

- **BP**: BP has rebranded itself as a company focused on delivering energy solutions that support a low-carbon future. It is investing heavily in wind, solar, and bioenergy, and has established a target of 50 gigawatts (GW) of renewable energy capacity by 2030.

- **Shell**: Shell's New Energies division is focused on scaling up renewable power generation, expanding its electric vehicle charging network, and exploring the potential of hydrogen. By 2030, Shell aims to become a leading electricity provider, with a focus on green energy solutions.

Chapter 3
Decarbonization and Reducing Carbon Footprint

3.1 Carbon Capture, Utilization, and Storage (CCUS)

CCUS technology is emerging as one of the most critical tools for reducing emissions from fossil fuel operations. CCUS involves capturing carbon dioxide (CO_2) emissions from industrial processes or directly from the atmosphere, transporting it, and storing it underground in geological formations. This prevents CO_2 from being released into the atmosphere, thereby mitigating its impact on global warming.

In addition to storage, captured carbon can also be used in **enhanced oil recovery (EOR)**, where CO_2 is injected into oil reservoirs to increase production. This process both reduces emissions and boosts oil output, creating a win-win for oil companies.

Many oil and gas companies are investing in large-scale CCUS projects, with several pilot programs already underway. For example, **ExxonMobil** and **Chevron** have invested in projects that aim to capture millions of tons of CO_2 annually from their operations and store it underground.

3.2 Improving Operational Efficiency

Decarbonization is not only about capturing emissions but also about preventing them in the first place. Oil and gas companies can improve the efficiency of their operations through:

- **Energy Efficiency**: Upgrading equipment, improving insulation, and optimizing processes to reduce the energy consumed during extraction, refining, and transportation.
- **Digitalization**: By implementing digital technologies such as artificial intelligence (AI), Internet of Things (IoT) sensors, and data analytics, companies can monitor energy use in real-time, identify inefficiencies, and optimize their operations.

For instance, **Chevron** is using digital twins—virtual models of physical assets that simulate real-world conditions—to monitor and optimize its offshore platforms. This reduces energy consumption and minimizes emissions.

3.3 Electrification of Operations

Electrifying oil and gas operations is another strategy to reduce emissions. This involves replacing fossil fuel-powered equipment with electric alternatives that run on renewable energy. For example, upstream oil rigs can be powered by renewable electricity, and electric vehicles (EVs) can replace diesel-powered trucks and machinery used in oil fields.

By electrifying operations, companies can significantly reduce their **scope 1 emissions** (direct emissions from owned or controlled sources) and contribute to the overall decarbonization of their business.

Chapter 4
Hydrogen as a Clean Fuel Source

4.1 Hydrogen Overview

Hydrogen is increasingly being seen as a critical component of the energy transition. It is a versatile energy carrier that can be used in a range of applications, including transportation, heating, and industrial processes. When produced from renewable sources, hydrogen emits no carbon dioxide, making it an attractive alternative to fossil fuels.

Hydrogen can be used in **fuel cells** to power vehicles, generate electricity, or provide heat for buildings. It is also a potential solution for decarbonizing heavy industries, such as steel and cement production, where direct electrification is difficult.

4.2 Hydrogen Production Pathways

There are several ways to produce hydrogen, with varying environmental impacts:

- **Grey Hydrogen**: Produced from natural gas via **steam methane reforming (SMR)**, without capturing the resulting CO_2 emissions. This is the most common and cheapest method but has a high carbon footprint.

- **Blue Hydrogen**: Produced from natural gas, but with the CO_2 emissions captured and stored using CCUS technology. This reduces its carbon footprint significantly compared to grey hydrogen.

- **Green Hydrogen**: Produced using **electrolysis**, a process that uses renewable electricity to split water into hydrogen and oxygen. This is the cleanest form of hydrogen but is currently more expensive than grey and blue hydrogen.

4.3 Hydrogen Partnerships

Scaling hydrogen production and infrastructure will require collaboration between governments, industry leaders, and renewable energy providers. Several oil and gas companies are already partnering with governments and research institutions to explore hydrogen's potential.

For example, **TotalEnergies** has partnered with **Engie** to produce green hydrogen for industrial use, while **Shell** is leading the development of **Hydrogen Valleys**—integrated ecosystems where hydrogen production, storage, and consumption are combined in one geographic location.

Chapter 5
Strategic Partnerships and Collaborations

5.1 Collaborating with Renewable Energy Companies

Partnerships between oil and gas companies and renewable energy firms can accelerate the pace of the energy transition. These collaborations allow both parties to share expertise, reduce costs, and scale up projects more efficiently.

For example, **Equinor**, Norway's state-owned oil company, has partnered with renewable energy developers to build offshore wind farms. These projects leverage Equinor's expertise in offshore drilling and infrastructure while allowing it to diversify into renewables.

Joint ventures are also becoming more common. In the U.K., **BP** and **Equinor** have formed a partnership to develop offshore wind projects, with plans to supply power to over 2 million homes by 2025.

5.2 Government and Policy Collaboration

Oil and gas companies must work closely with governments to shape the policy frameworks needed to support the energy transition. This includes advocating for incentives such as tax credits for renewable energy investments, funding for CCUS and hydrogen projects, and research and development support.

Public-private partnerships can also unlock significant funding for clean energy projects. For example, the U.S. government's **Infrastructure Investment and Jobs Act** provides billions of dollars for clean energy infrastructure, including carbon capture and hydrogen projects. Oil and gas companies that actively engage in these partnerships can benefit from early access to government grants and contracts.

5.3 Academic and Research Collaborations

Collaboration with universities and research institutions is crucial for advancing the technologies needed for the energy transition. These partnerships foster innovation in areas such as battery storage, advanced biofuels, and next-generation solar and wind technologies.

For instance, **Chevron** has partnered with **Stanford University** to research low-carbon technologies, while **Shell** collaborates with the **University of Amsterdam** on green hydrogen and renewable energy storage solutions.

Chapter 6
Sustainable Business Models and Financial Innovation

6.1 Sustainable Financing

Sustainable finance is becoming an increasingly important tool for oil and gas companies looking to fund their energy transition strategies. Investors are increasingly favoring companies that demonstrate strong **Environmental, Social, and Governance (ESG)** credentials. As a result, oil and gas companies are issuing **green bonds** and **sustainability-linked loans** to fund renewable energy and carbon reduction projects.

Green bonds are specifically tied to environmentally friendly projects, such as wind farms or solar power installations. **Sustainability-linked loans** are tied to a company's ability to meet specific sustainability targets, such as reducing emissions or increasing renewable energy capacity. If these targets are not met, the company may face financial penalties or higher interest rates.

For example, **Repsol**, a major Spanish oil company, issued its first green bond in 2021 to raise capital for low-carbon projects. Similarly, **TotalEnergies** has used sustainability-linked financing to support its energy transition initiatives.

6.2 Circular Economy

The **circular economy** is a sustainable business model that focuses on minimizing waste, reusing resources, and creating closed-loop systems where materials are continuously recycled. Oil and gas companies can integrate circular economy principles into their operations by reducing waste, using byproducts more efficiently, and finding ways to repurpose CO_2.

For example, **ExxonMobil** is investing in technologies that capture waste heat from industrial processes and use it to generate electricity, thereby improving energy efficiency. Additionally, some companies are exploring ways to recycle water used in hydraulic fracturing and repurpose CO_2 emissions for commercial products like building materials.

6.3 Long-Term Value Creation

Oil and gas companies must shift from focusing on short-term profits to creating long-term value. This means balancing economic performance with environmental sustainability and social responsibility. Companies that invest in clean energy technologies, reduce their carbon footprints, and prioritize ESG principles will be better positioned to attract investors and maintain profitability in the long term.

The focus on long-term value creation is already influencing company strategies. **Eni**, Italy's state-owned energy giant, has set a goal of becoming carbon-neutral by 2050 and is investing heavily in renewables and bioenergy. Similarly, **Equinor** is aiming to reduce its emissions by 50% by 2030, with a long-term goal of becoming a net-zero company by 2050.

Chapter 7
Workforce Transition and Reskilling

7.1 Reskilling the Workforce

The energy transition will require significant reskilling and retraining of the workforce to ensure that employees are prepared for new roles in renewable energy, carbon capture, and hydrogen production. Oil and gas companies must invest in training programs to upskill their workforce and ensure that they have the expertise needed to manage and operate clean energy infrastructure.

By providing educational opportunities and retraining programs, companies can retain valuable employees while ensuring they are equipped to contribute to the company's future in the low-carbon economy.

For example, **Schlumberger**, one of the world's largest oilfield services companies, has launched a comprehensive reskilling program to train its workforce for the transition to cleaner energy technologies. The program focuses on renewable energy, carbon capture, and digital technologies that optimize energy efficiency.

7.2 Attracting New Talent

Attracting younger, sustainability-focused talent is crucial for oil and gas companies to remain competitive in the evolving energy market. The younger workforce is increasingly drawn to companies that prioritize environmental sustainability, corporate responsibility, and social impact.

To attract this talent, oil and gas companies need to promote their efforts in renewable energy, carbon reduction, and clean technology development. Additionally, offering employees the chance to work on cutting-edge clean energy projects can help build excitement and engagement within the company.

7.3 Employee Engagement in the Energy Transition

Employee engagement is critical for the successful implementation of an energy transition strategy. Oil and gas companies must create a culture of sustainability and innovation by involving employees in the decision-making process and encouraging them to contribute ideas.

This can be achieved by creating **sustainability task forces** or **innovation labs**, where employees from different departments can collaborate on projects that advance the company's clean energy goals. By fostering a culture of innovation, companies can empower their workforce to take ownership of the energy transition and drive meaningful change.

Conclusion

The energy transition is not just an opportunity for oil and gas companies to adapt to a changing market; it is a necessity for long-term survival. As the world moves toward a low-carbon future, oil and gas companies must play a leading role in developing and deploying the technologies and infrastructure that will enable this shift.

By investing in renewable energy, embracing decarbonization strategies, fostering strategic partnerships, and reskilling their workforce, oil and gas companies can remain competitive while contributing to a cleaner, more sustainable world. The transition will not be easy, but those companies that act now and take proactive steps toward decarbonization will be well-positioned for success in the years to come.

Glossary: Energy Transition Strategies for Oil and Gas Companies

1. **Biofuels**: Renewable fuels derived from organic materials such as plants, agricultural waste, or algae, used to reduce reliance on fossil fuels in transportation and energy generation.

2. **Carbon Capture and Storage (CCS)**: A technology that captures carbon dioxide emissions from industrial sources and stores them underground to prevent their release into the atmosphere.

3. **Carbon Intensity**: The amount of carbon dioxide emissions produced per unit of energy or fuel consumed, used as a measure of the environmental impact of different energy sources.

4. **Carbon Offset**: A reduction in emissions of carbon dioxide or other greenhouse gases made in order to compensate for emissions produced elsewhere.

5. **Carbon Pricing**: A market-based approach to controlling carbon emissions by placing a monetary value on the cost of emitting carbon, typically through carbon taxes or cap-and-trade systems.

6. **Circular Economy**: An economic model focused on minimizing waste and making the most of resources by reusing, recycling, and repurposing materials throughout their lifecycle.

7. **Climate Risk**: The potential financial and operational impacts on a company due to the effects of climate change, including extreme weather events and regulatory changes.

8. **Corporate Sustainability**: Business practices that focus on creating long-term value by taking into account the environmental, social, and economic impacts of a company's operations.

9. **Decarbonization**: The process of reducing carbon dioxide emissions from energy production, transportation, and industrial processes, typically by shifting to renewable energy sources and increasing efficiency.

10. **Direct Air Capture (DAC)**: A technology that captures carbon dioxide directly from the atmosphere for storage or reuse in various industrial processes.

11. **Energy Efficiency**: The practice of using less energy to perform the same task or produce the same outcome, reducing overall energy consumption and emissions.

12. **Energy Mix**: The combination of different energy sources—such as fossil fuels, renewables, and nuclear energy—that a country or company uses to meet its energy needs.

13. **Energy Storage**: Technologies used to store energy for later use, such as batteries or pumped hydro storage, critical for balancing supply and demand in renewable energy systems.

14. **Environmental, Social, and Governance (ESG)**: A set of criteria used to evaluate a company's operations and performance in terms of sustainability, ethical practices, and corporate governance.

15. **Flaring**: The burning of natural gas that is released as a byproduct during oil extraction, often due to a lack of infrastructure for capturing or using the gas.

16. **Fossil Fuels**: Non-renewable energy sources such as coal, oil, and natural gas, formed from the remains of ancient plants and animals, and major contributors to greenhouse gas emissions.

17. **Fuel Switching**: The process of changing from one energy source to another, typically from fossil fuels to cleaner alternatives, as part of a decarbonization strategy.

18. **Geothermal Energy**: A renewable energy source that uses heat from the Earth's core to generate electricity or provide direct heating.

19. **Green Hydrogen**: Hydrogen produced through the electrolysis of water using renewable energy, considered a key component in reducing emissions in hard-to-decarbonize sectors.

20. **Greenhouse Gas (GHG)**: Gases that trap heat in the Earth's atmosphere, contributing to global warming. Key GHGs include carbon dioxide (CO_2), methane (CH_4), and nitrous oxide (N_2O).

21. **Hydrogen Economy**: A future energy system where hydrogen is a primary fuel for transportation, industrial processes, and power generation, replacing fossil fuels to reduce emissions.

22. **Hydropower**: Renewable energy generated by harnessing the energy of moving water, typically through dams or turbines, to produce electricity.

23. **Intermittency**: The variability in energy output from renewable sources such as solar and wind, which are dependent on weather conditions and time of day.

24. **Just Transition**: An approach to the energy transition that ensures the shift to renewable energy is equitable, protecting jobs, communities, and vulnerable populations.

25. **Methane Emissions**: The release of methane, a potent greenhouse gas, during the production and transportation of natural gas and oil.

26. **Methanol**: A cleaner-burning fuel that can be produced from natural gas, biomass, or carbon dioxide and used as a transition fuel for maritime and industrial applications.

27. **Net Zero**: Achieving a balance between the amount of greenhouse gases emitted and the amount removed from the atmosphere, often the goal for companies and countries in mitigating climate change.

28. **Offshore Wind Energy**: The generation of electricity from wind turbines located in bodies of water, which tend to have stronger and more consistent winds than onshore locations.

29. **Oil Sands**: A mixture of sand, clay, water, and bitumen found in regions such as Canada, from which oil is extracted, often requiring energy-intensive processes.

30. **Photovoltaics (PV)**: Solar panels that convert sunlight directly into electricity through the use of semiconducting materials.

31. **Power Purchase Agreement (PPA)**: A long-term contract between an energy producer and a buyer, typically for the purchase of renewable electricity at a pre-agreed price.

32. **Renewable Energy**: Energy generated from sources that are naturally replenished, such as wind, solar, hydro, geothermal, and biomass, without depleting the Earth's resources.

33. **Renewable Portfolio Standard (RPS)**: A policy that requires utilities to source a certain percentage of their energy from renewable sources, helping drive the adoption of renewables.

34. **Renewable Natural Gas (RNG)**: Biogas that has been processed to meet natural gas standards, produced from organic materials like agricultural waste, landfills, or wastewater treatment plants.

35. **Resilience**: The ability of energy systems and infrastructure to withstand and recover from disruptions, including those caused by extreme weather, cyber-attacks, or supply chain challenges.

36. **Scope 1, 2, and 3 Emissions**: Categories of greenhouse gas emissions; Scope 1 refers to direct emissions from company-owned operations, Scope 2 includes indirect emissions from energy use, and Scope 3 covers emissions from the entire value chain, including suppliers and customers.

37. **Smart Grid**: An electricity network that uses digital technology to monitor and manage energy flows, enabling more efficient use of energy and integration of renewable sources.

38. **Solar Energy**: Energy harnessed from the sun, typically through photovoltaic cells or solar thermal systems, to generate electricity or heat.

39. **Stranded Assets**: Investments or resources that become obsolete or devalued due to changes in the market or regulatory environment, such as fossil fuel reserves in a decarbonized world.

40. **Sustainability Reporting**: The disclosure of a company's environmental, social, and governance (ESG) performance, including actions taken to reduce emissions and manage climate risks.

41. **Tidal Energy**: A form of renewable energy that generates power from the rise and fall of ocean tides, using turbines or other technology to convert the movement of water into electricity.

42. **Transition Fuel**: A lower-emission fuel, such as natural gas or methanol, used as a temporary solution to bridge the gap between high-emission fossil fuels and renewable energy.

43. **Upstream**: The part of the oil and gas industry that involves exploration, drilling, and production of crude oil and natural gas.

44. **Waste-to-Energy**: A process that generates energy from the combustion of waste materials, contributing to both waste management and energy production.

45. **Water Electrolysis**: A process that uses electricity to split water into hydrogen and oxygen, producing green hydrogen when powered by renewable energy.

46. **Wind Energy**: The process of generating electricity from wind using turbines that convert kinetic energy from the wind into electrical energy.

47. **Zero-Emission Vehicle (ZEV)**: A vehicle that emits no exhaust pollutants from the onboard source of power, typically referring to electric vehicles powered by batteries or fuel cells.

48. **Zero-Routine Flaring**: A commitment by oil and gas companies to eliminate the practice of flaring natural gas during routine operations, reducing methane emissions and waste.

49. **Zonal Pricing**: A method of electricity pricing that reflects the cost of delivering power to different areas, accounting for congestion in transmission lines and the availability of renewable energy.

50. **Zoning**: The regulation of land use and development, often relevant in the siting of renewable energy projects, such as wind farms or solar arrays, to minimize environmental impacts and conflicts with other land uses.

www.ingramcontent.com/pod-product-compliance
Lightning Source LLC
Chambersburg PA
CBHW030041230526
45472CB00002B/624